Your Child a[illegible]

Working at home with your child can be a very enjoyable shared experience. It is also an invaluable part of his or her education.

This book is designed to give a selection of tasks which most 7-year-olds should be able to perform. It is for children in Year Two of the National Curriculum.

The activities are closely linked to the National Curriculum and are based on the three core subjects, Mathematics, English and Science. Many disciplines interact in the learning process. For example, a skill developed through Science will often contribute to those needed in English, or a task undertaken in Maths may also develop language skills. The [illegible] for Parents over the page include simple symbols to show which subject skills are practised in each activity.

M Maths E English S Science

Help your child to get the best out of this book by:

- finding a quiet time when you are both relaxed and undisturbed for maximum concentration. Enjoy the time together and the activity.
- letting your child help select an activity.
- talking about each activity, exchanging opinions, working out problems. Developing speaking and listening skills will help all other areas of learning.
- trying to finish on a good point, before your child gets tired. Let him or her control the pace.
- always giving plenty of praise and encouragement. Everyone responds well if they feel they are succeeding.

Rhona Whiteford and Jim Fitzsimmons
Illustrated by David Farris

Headway • Hodder & Stoughton

NOTES FOR PARENTS

Pages 4-5 Counting to 100 M E

These exercises develop an awareness of patterns in numbers and link this to the learning of the multiplication tables in a practical and fun way.

Page 6 Multiplication facts M E

Practice in finding the related numbers in the multiplication tables. In multiplication (as with addition), all the numbers can be swapped e.g. 3 x 2 =6 and 2 x 3 =6.

Page 7 Measuring in centimetres M E

A chance to use centimetres (standard units of measurement) and conduct a simple survey, recording the results on a chart. Encourage the child to make an estimate of the length, then check it. Praise any attempt, as more accurate estimation comes with practice.

Page 8 Calculator Colin M

This activity gives practice in recognition of number bonds to 20 and in the place of tens and units in numbers. It is a good opportunity to develop calculator skills and can be used as a speed and accuracy test for those familiar with a calculator.

Page 9 Weighing M S E

Practical practice in weighing materials. Discuss how the ingredients change as they are mixed together and subjected to heat. This is an important observation for science.

Page 10 Time M E

A practical opportunity to experience a limited time period in order to develop a fuller understanding of the concept. The results are recorded in chart form as this is an important tool in the application of maths.

Page 11 Clothes show M E

This offers two short surveys which can then be analysed.

Page 12 Sharing M E

This is a visual introduction to division which can be easily done in a practical way at tea time. Encourage your child to circle or cross out items to help them complete the activity.

Page 13 Letter patterns E

Practice in letter patterns to develop skills towards cursive writing. Do encourage neat presentation and a pride in all work.

Pages 14-15 Hometown E M

This plan is designed to promote discussion and observation and give opportunity to formulate and follow instructions and directions. This will help towards the development of logical thought. Thinking up road names and adding more features to the plan will stretch imagination.

Page 16 A winter story E

This is a useful planning and discussion device for organising thoughts and ideas when writing a story.

Page 17 Listening to music E

This is designed to focus the child's attention on the music and develop listening skills.

Pages 18-19 Spelling E

These exercises give practice in spelling words with the common consonant digraphs (ch, sh, th). Encourage the 'Look/cover/write' strategy as it aids development of memory and retention of words.

Page 20 Reading E

This simple comprehension exercise helps logical thought, careful reading and memory development.

Page 21 Letter writing E

This is an imaginative opportunity to learn how to write a letter.

Pages 22-23 What weather! S E

Here are several activities to help collect and record information about weather. Discuss the results so that your child can see how information can be analysed and used.

Page 24 Design brief S

Here is a chance to discover if your family have any building dreams that can be analysed and planned on this sheet. Ask your child to think about the suitability of the materials for different parts of the building.

Page 25 Friction S E

This is a simple test to observe the effects of friction caused by different surfaces. Discuss the relationship between the surface and the distance the toy travelled.

Page 26 Decay S E

This experiment is for observation of changes in materials over a period of time. Discuss how our household rubbish and industrial waste is processed.

Page 27 Magnetic energy S E

A simple survey to sort out materials which are affected by a magnet, and an exploration of magnetic energy. At this level ask the child to formulate simple hypotheses, such as 'I think my magnet is powerful enough to hold a chain of 40 paper-clips'. Then test this and analyse the results.

Pages 28-29 Hot and cold S E

These activities about temperature and insulation encourage exploration, questioning and analysis of findings.

Pages 30-31 On the animal trail S

These activities inspire questions about how other species live and also help develop research skills.

Counting to 100

Complete the rows of numbers, each in its own colour.
Use felt pens or pencil crayons.

Count as you write.

1									10
11									20
21									30
31									40
41									50
51									60
61									70
71									80
81									90
91									100

What do you notice about the numbers in each column?

Colour every 2nd square.
Use the same colour.
What do you notice?

1	2	3	4	5	6	7	8	9	10
11	12	13	14	15	16	17	18	19	20
21	22	23	24	25	26	27	28	29	30
31	32	33	34	35	36	37	38	39	40
41	42	43	44	45	46	47	48	49	50
51	52	53	54	55	56	57	58	59	60
61	62	63	64	65	66	67	68	69	70
71	72	73	74	75	76	77	78	79	80
81	82	83	84	85	86	87	88	89	90
91	92	93	94	95	96	97	98	99	100

1	2	3	4	5	6	7	8	9	10
11	12	13	14	15	16	17	18	19	20
21	22	23	24	25	26	27	28	29	30
31	32	33	34	35	36	37	38	39	40
41	42	43	44	45	46	47	48	49	50
51	52	53	54	55	56	57	58	59	60
61	62	63	64	65	66	67	68	69	70
71	72	73	74	75	76	77	78	79	80
81	82	83	84	85	86	87	88	89	90
91	92	93	94	95	96	97	98	99	100

Colour every 3rd square.
Use a different colour.

Colour every 4th square.

1	2	3	4	5	6	7	8	9	10
11	12	13	14	15	16	17	18	19	20
21	22	23	24	25	26	27	28	29	30
31	32	33	34	35	36	37	38	39	40
41	42	43	44	45	46	47	48	49	50
51	52	53	54	55	56	57	58	59	60
61	62	63	64	65	66	67	68	69	70
71	72	73	74	75	76	77	78	79	80
81	82	83	84	85	86	87	88	89	90
91	92	93	94	95	96	97	98	99	100

Multiplication facts

Write the missing facts in the white circles.
We've done the first one for you.

Measuring in centimetres

Look at the ruler at the edge of this page. It is 20 cm long. Can you find 5 things which are shorter than it? Look at the object and guess its length. Then check by measuring. How good was your guess?

cm 1 2 3 4 5 6 7 8 9 10 11 12 13 14 15 16 17 18 19 20

item	my estimate	actual measurement
1		
2		
3		
4		
5		

Now look for 5 things shorter than 5 cm.

item	my estimate	actual measurement
1		
2		
3		
4		
5		

My guesses were:

good ☐ quite good ☐ not too good ☐

Calculator Colin

10	+	1	=	
10	+	2	=	
10	+	3	=	
10	+	4	=	
10	+	5	=	
10	+	6	=	
10	+	7	=	
10	+	8	=	
10	+	9	=	
10	+	10	=	

How long did it take you?

It took me ☐ minutes.

Weighing

Muffins for tea...

You will need

- 250g wholewheat flour
- 110g brown sugar
- 110g crunchy breakfast cereal
- 3 level teaspoons baking powder
- $\frac{1}{4}$ teaspoon salt
- 1 egg
- 300ml milk
- 75ml oil
- 2 tablespoons of any of these: chopped apple, nuts, sultanas.

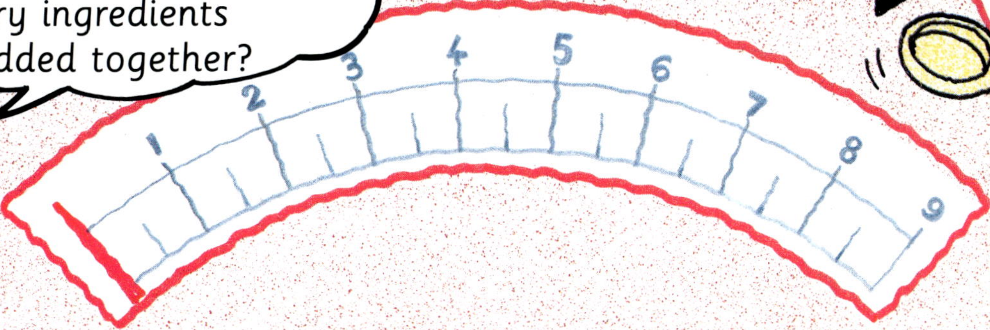

How to make them:

1. Beat egg, then add milk and oil. Mix.
2. Add all flour, cereal, sugar, baking powder and salt. Mix.
3. Add nuts or whatever. Mix.
4. Spoon the mixture into bun tins.
5. Bake at 400°F/200°C for 20 to 25 minutes.

First estimate the weights you need, then weigh on the scales for accuracy.

What happened to each of the materials as you mixed them?
What were they like when you cooked (added heat to) them?

Time

How many times can you do these things in one minute?
Guess first, then try it out.
Ask someone to time you while you count.

action	my estimate	actual result
hop on one leg		
write your name		
bounce a ball		
touch your toes		
ride round garden on a bike		

What can you draw in this space in 5 minutes?
Keep going with more ideas until the time is up.

Clothes show

Do this simple survey on our models. We've done Sally for you.
Then analyse your family's colour scheme today.

Colours worn

Name	blue	yellow	green	red	white	orange	pink	brown
Sally		✓	✓		✓		✓	
Anita								
Yogesh								
Sean								
Total								

Yogesh

Anita

My family

Colours worn

Name	blue	yellow	green	red	white	orange	pink	brown
Total								

Sean

Sally

Sharing

Put a tick in the right box.	Yes	No
Can each child have 2 jellies?	☐	☐
Can each child have 1 packet of crisps?	☐	☐
Can each child have 2 cakes?	☐	☐
Can each child have 3 sausages?	☐	☐
Can each child have 3 biscuits?	☐	☐
Can each child have 1 sandwich?	☐	☐

Ask a grown-up to check your answers.

Letter patterns

Try these patterns without lifting your pencil off the page.

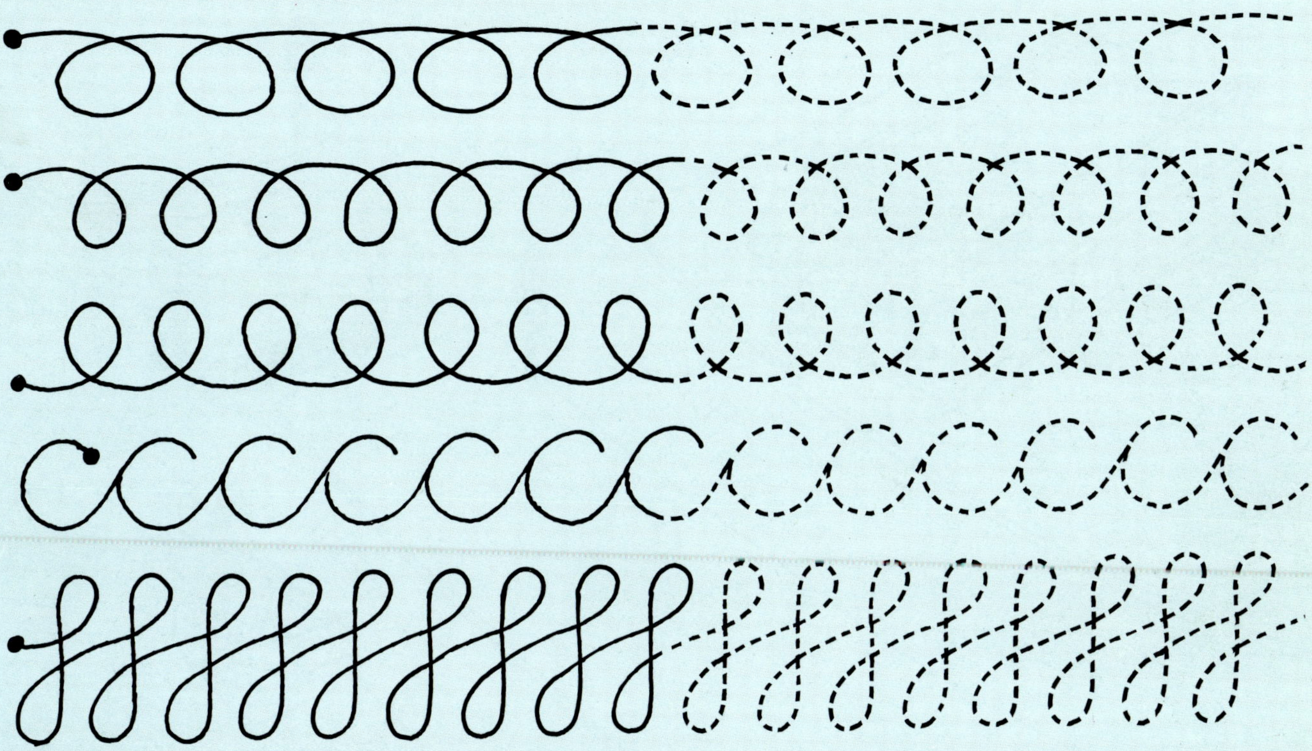

Now design your own wallpaper using letter patterns. Make it a repeating pattern using different coloured pencil crayons.

Hometown

First make up road names for Hometown and write them on the plan. Where would you like to live? Choose a place, and draw your house on the plan.

Lane
Gran's
Cinema
Park
School
Place
Street
Baths
Can you give someone else directions on this plan without pointing? Use words like 'right', 'left' and 'straight on'.

A winter story

Plan a wonderful winter story on this story board. Write short notes about what will happen in the story.

characters

place / time

main event

opening

ending

Listening to music

Listen to any piece of music carefully, then write or draw what it makes you think about.

Spelling

<u>ch</u>erry

_ _urch

_ _ip

_ _erry

_ _in

_ _air

_ _at

_ _oose

_ _ill

_ _est

<u>th</u>umb

mo_ _er

pa_ _

_ _is

_ _ere

bro_ _er

_ _at

ba_ _

_ _ick

_ _e

_ _umb

a	s	h	i	p	b	c
d	e	s	h	a	r	e
s	h	u	t	f	g	m
n	i	j	s	h	o	w
k	s	h	a	r	p	n
t	x	s	h	e	l	l

Practise the words on these pages and try to write them down here.

Look at the word, then cover it and try to write it.	check ✔ or ✘	write again

Reading

Read the sentences carefully and follow the instructions.

The mice that do not like cheese have short tails.
Colour the mice that do like cheese red.

The elves which are good carry mushrooms.
Colour the bad elves blue.

The fish that have been fed swim on the bottom of the tank.
Colour the hungry fish yellow.

Read and follow the instructions to colour in the boy.

Colour his hat blue, then give him a yellow shirt.
Colour his shoes green, and give him red trousers.
He has brown hair and a black belt.

Letter writing

Imagine you are writing to ask for details about a Space holiday. List the sort of things you would like to see, and the planets you would like to visit.

Write your address here.

Dear

Yours faithfully

What weather!

Make a rain gauge

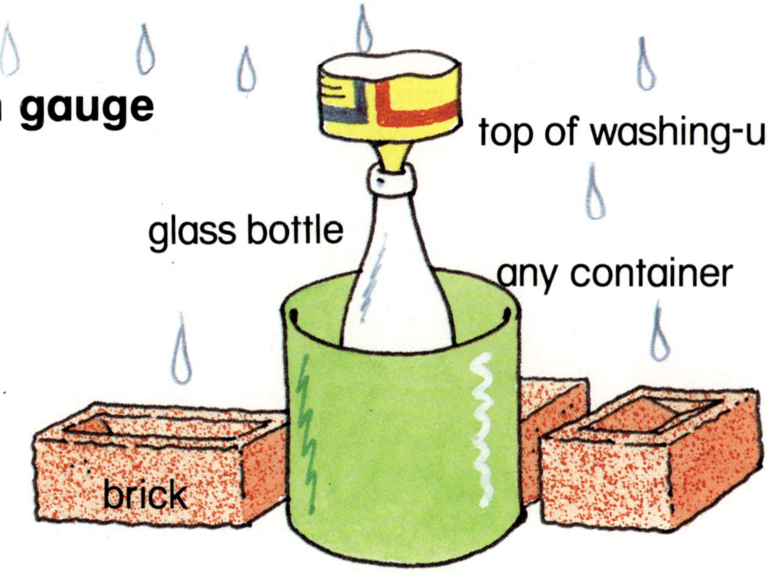

Put it outside in an unsheltered spot.

A week's rainfall

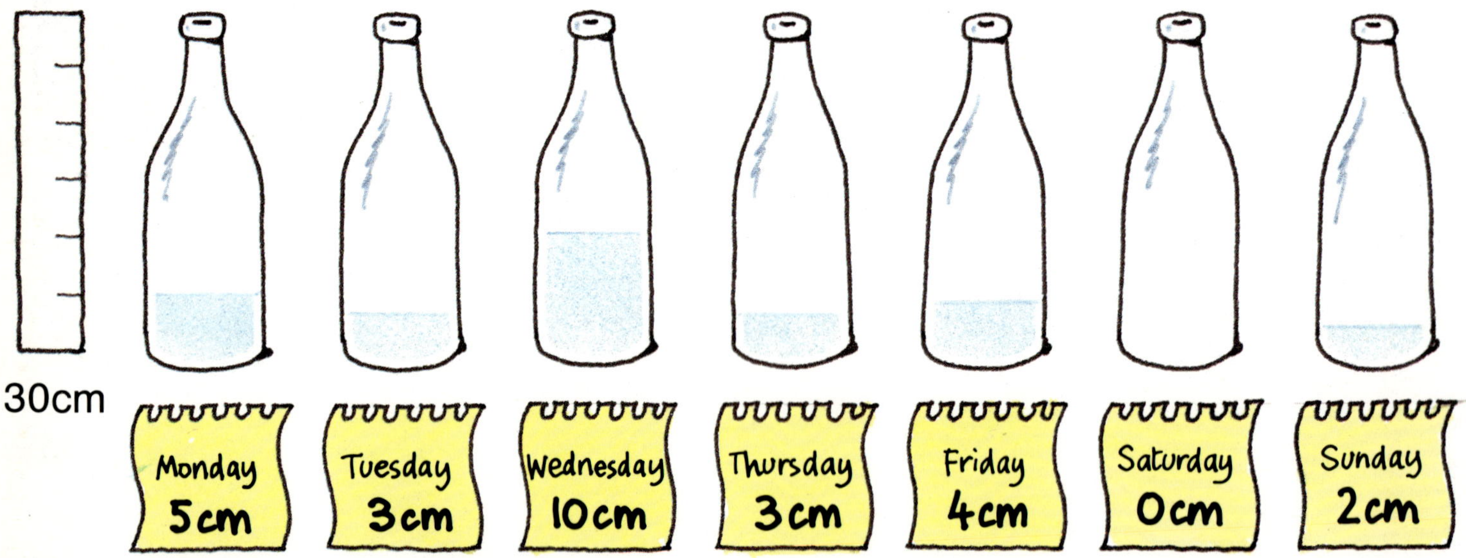

Measure the rainfall for a week.

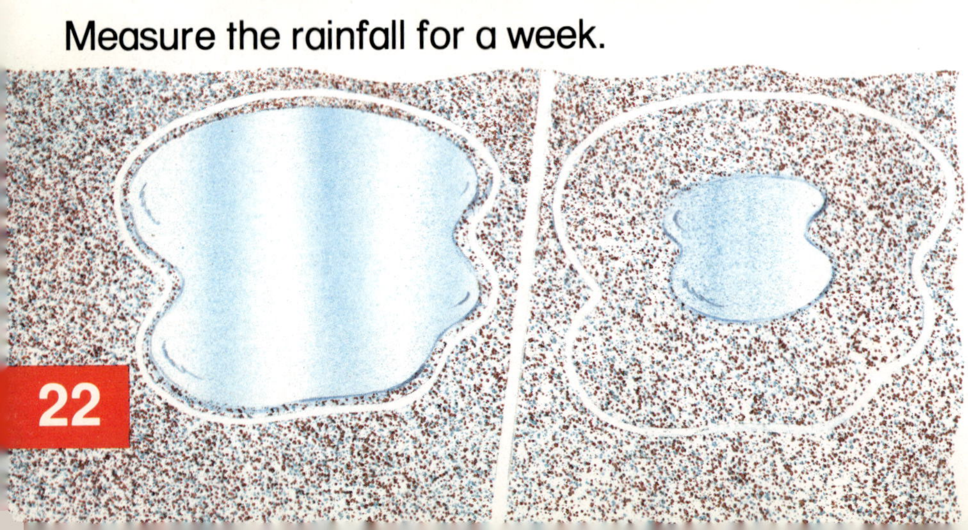

Puddles

Where do they go to?
Chalk round a puddle and
leave for one hour.
What dries up the water?
What dries washing on the line

Make a wind-sock with a pair of tights.

Attach the tights to a simple wire hoop and tie to a pole.
Make a note of the wind direction each day.
(Use a compass to find out where north is.)

Use this chart to record the week's weather.

Weather Record

	Rainfall	Wind direction	Temperature (use a thermometer)
Monday			
Tuesday			
Wednesday			
Thursday			
Friday			
Saturday			
Sunday			

Design brief

Design a perfect house for your family. Ask them what they would like.

Location ______________________________

Materials ______________________________

Special needs ______________________________

Sketch the house here.

Friction

Have you ever had problems pushing your pram across the lawn or zooming a car across the carpet?

Your problem is FRICTION!

Friction occurs when two surfaces grip each other and stop free movement. When you slip across a tiled floor wearing socks there is little friction between the two smooth surfaces.

Try giving the toy a gentle push on each of the following surfaces. Then try a strong push.
Measure how far it travels each time.

Surface	Distance travelled cm: Gentle push	Strong push
lawn		
carpet		
smooth floor		
table		
outside path		

What did you notice about the different surfaces?

Decay

Everything changes with time!
...or does it?

Collect
• 6 plastic containers • cling film • labels • 6 different materials such as:

orange peel

bread

piece of potato

apple core

ketchup

nail + water

Talk to parents, or read books, to find out how chemicals and moulds help change materials.

Put one in each container and seal the lid with cling film. Leave for 10 days, then look carefully to spot any changes. What did you notice?

Material	Changes
1	
2	
3	
4	
5	
6	

Magnetic energy

Find 5 things in your house that are attracted to a magnet. What do you notice about the material? Write them here. ➡

Make a paper-clip chain and lift it up using a magnet. How many did you lift?

☐ paper-clips

Can you lift metal things out of a jar of water without getting your hands wet?

yes ☐ no ☐

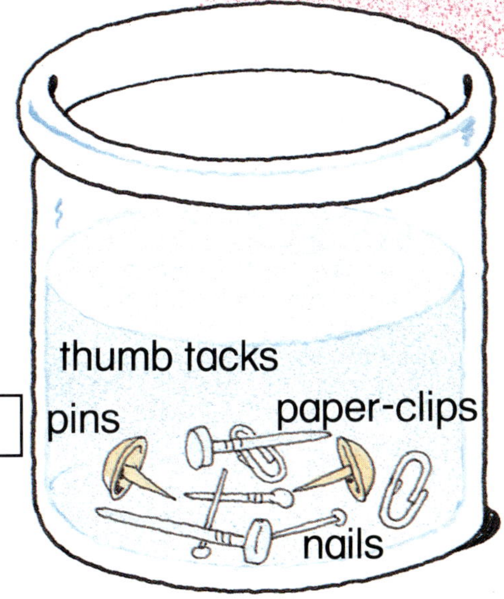

Make a fishing game to play with your magnet.

Add up the numbers on the fish you catch to get your total.

Hot and cold

What things make you feel hot and what things make you feel cold?

Which colours make you think of heat or cold?
Try to match these shades with your pens.

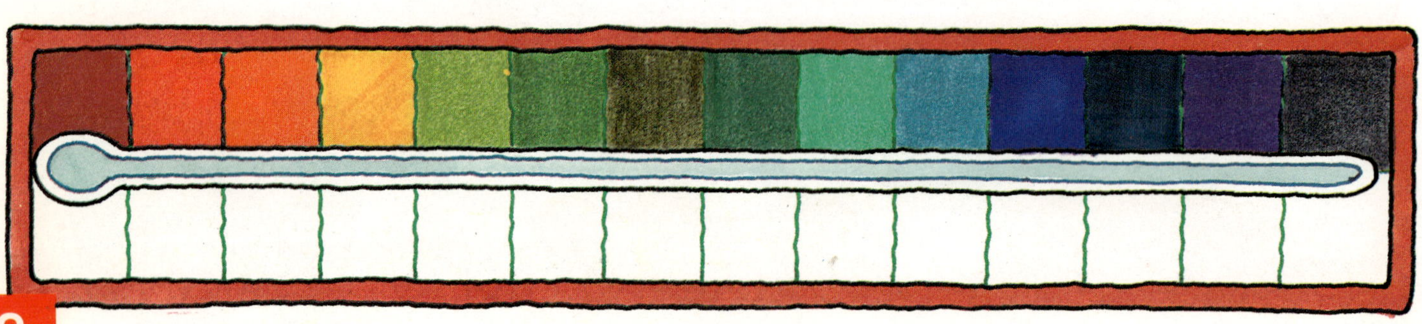

What keeps heat in?
Find 3 or more plastic bottles .
Get an adult to fill them with warm water.

1 Wrap each bottle with a different material.
2 Leave for 1 hour.
3 Test with hand or thermometer to see which has stayed warm.
4 Repeat with different materials to find best insulator.

Materials

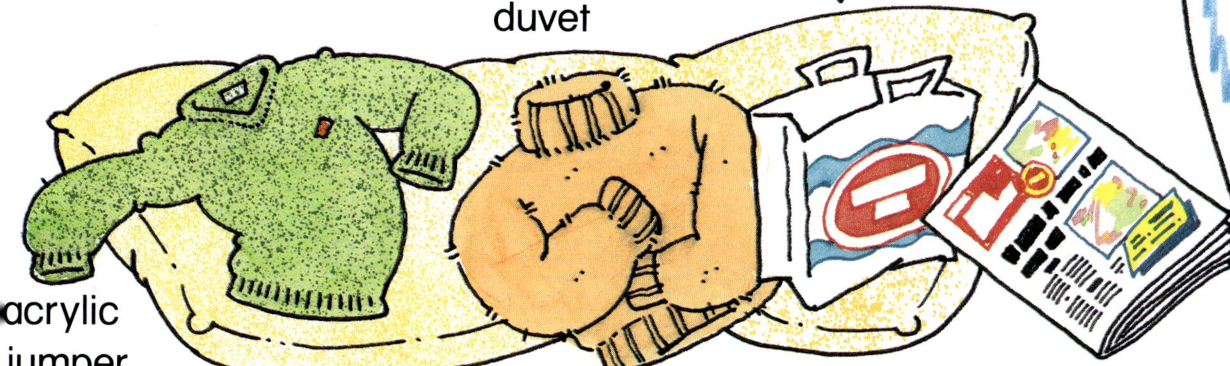

Covered with	temperature °C before	after	hand test warm	quite warm	cold
1					
2					
3					
4					
5					
6					

On the animal trail

Where would you expect to see these animals?

elephant

lion

guinea-pig

goat

kestrel

badger

blackbird

mallard

Try visiting these places

- pet shop
- library
- countryside
- safari park
- zoo
- wildlife park
- the garden

Draw your favourite animal here.

Colour the boxes which are true about this animal.

What it is

- mammal ☐
- reptile ☐
- bird ☐
- amphibian ☐
- fish ☐
- other ☐

Who it lives with

- alone ☐
- in a herd ☐
- as a family ☐

Where it lives

- mountain ☐
- jungle ☐
- underground ☐
- underwater ☐
- plain ☐
- other ☐

What it likes

- warmth ☐
- light ☐
- cold ☐
- dark ☐

Food it likes

- plants ☐
- animal ☐
- both ☐

HEADStart

A complete home-learning range.

When your child has completed this book, there are plenty of others to choose from the Headstart range.

Here is a selection:

Your Child at ...

Each of these books practises skills in English, Maths and Science.

- Your Child at 4
- Your Child at 5
- Your Child at 6
- Your Child at 7

Headstart 5-7

National Curriculum skills practice for children at Key Stage 1.

- Handwriting
- Reading & Writing
- Spelling
- Number
- Measuring & Shape
- Science

Test Practice (Age 7)

Give your child a head start in the national tests at Key Stage 1.

- English
- Maths 1
- Maths 2
- Maths 3
- Science
- Spelling

Headstart 7-9

National Curriculum skills practice for children at Key Stage 2.

- Handwriting
- Spelling
- English skills
- Number skills
- Maths skills
- Science

British Library Cataloguing in Publication Data
Whiteford, Rhona
Your Child at 7
I. Title II. Fitzsimmons, Jim
649

ISBN 0-340-59099-8

First published 1993
Impression number 10 9 8 7 6 5 4 3 2 1
Year 1998 1997 1996 1995 1994 1993

Printed in Hong Kong for the educational publishing division of Hodder & Stoughton Ltd, Mill Road, Dunton Green, Sevenoaks, Kent TN13 2YA by Colorcraft.

Photography: Roddy Paine, Tunbridge Wells.
The children in the photographs are wearing clothes in the Ladybird range, produced exclusively for Woolworths plc and available in selected stores.